Trains and Railroads

Words by Howard W. Kanetzke

Juvenile Publications Editor
State Historical Society of Wisconsin

RSVP
RAINTREE STECK-VAUGHN
PUBLISHERS
The Steck-Vaughn Company

Austin, Texas

Cover Photo: Santa Fe Southern Pacific Corp.

Library of Congress Number: 87-20813

 4 5 6 7 8 9   W   97 96 95 94 93 92

Library of Congress Cataloging in Publication Data

Kanetzke, Howard W.
   Trains and railroads.

   Bibliography: p. 47
   Summary: An introduction to the history of trains with a discussion of differnt kinds of trains and railroads and how they work.
   1. Railroads—Juvenile literature. [1. Railroads]
I. Title.
TF148.K36 1987   385   87-20813
ISBN 0-8172-3263-X hardcover library binding
ISBN 0-8114-8222-7 softcover binding

Trains and Railroads

The first railroads were in coal mines. They were used to move coal through the mines. The rails, or tracks, were made of wood. Miners loaded coal into small wooden cars. Workers or horses moved cars over the rails.

Soon people hooked cars together. That way more coal could be moved on each trip. Sometimes the rails ran from the mine to a river. At the river, the coal was loaded onto boats.

iron rail

wooden blocks

Later, the rails and the wheels of the cars were made of iron. Iron rails rested on wooden blocks. The rails were strong. They could carry heavy loads. But even strong horses could pull only a few cars at a time.

Then the steam
engine was invented.
The steam engine
could move heavier
loads. The first steam
engines did not move
on wheels. They stood
at one end of the
tracks. A rope or
chain ran from the
engine to the cars.
The engine pulled the
cars out of the mines.

Catch Me Who Can

Puffing Billy

This first steam engine to run on rails was built in 1804 by Richard Trevithick. He also built a steam engine called Catch Me Who Can. It ran on a round track near London, England. People came to see it. Everyone wanted a ride.

Another famous engine was called Puffing Billy. It was built in 1813 by William Hedley. It was used to pull coal cars.

Locomotion

The first railroad to have a steam engine was in England. The railroad was built by George Stephenson in 1821. It ran between Stockton and Darlington. The tracks were 25 miles long. The steam engine was called Locomotion. Its cars carried goods and people.

In 1829, Stephenson built the Rocket. It was the most famous steam engine of all. It was faster than all other engines. It traveled about 30 miles per hour.

Rocket

People worked
hard to build the first
railroads. Trains could
not go up and down
hills. So workers had
to cut through hills.
Sometimes they dug
tunnels for the trains.
Many miles of railroad
tracks were built
during the 1800s.

People all over the world began to build railroads. A railroad was finished across the United States in 1869. Workers laid tracks from the east and west. They met in Utah. A celebration was held. A golden spike was used where the tracks met. Now trains could travel from one coast to the other.

cowcatcher

At one time, all railroads in America used similar engines. These engines had "cowcatchers" at the front. These pushed things on the track out of the way. Some engines were painted brightly. Others were black.

Union Pacific Big Boy engine

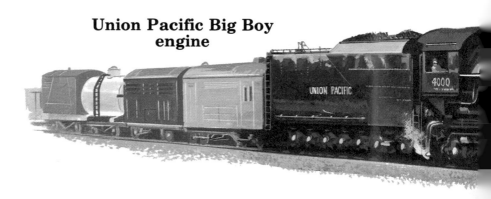

Mallard

One engine, the Mallard, looked different. It holds the world speed record for steam engines. It traveled at 126 miles per hour (202 kilometers per hour) in 1938. The Big Boy engine is one of the biggest engines ever built.

The land a railroad track runs on is called a right-of-way. The steel tracks rest on wooden strips called ties. The wheels of the train have ridges, or lips. The lips fit over the tracks.

Sometimes tracks meet or cross each other. This place is called a junction, or switching point. At junctions, trains can switch from one set of tracks to another. There are many junctions outside big railroad stations.

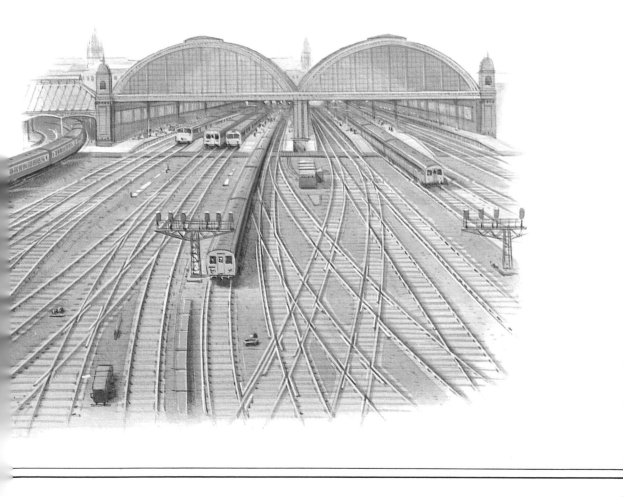

semaphore
signals

Railroad people plan when and on
which tracks each train will run. There are
signals along every railroad track. They tell
the trains if they should go ahead or stop.
Early signals were called semaphore
signals. They were worked by hand.
Modern signals work by electricity.

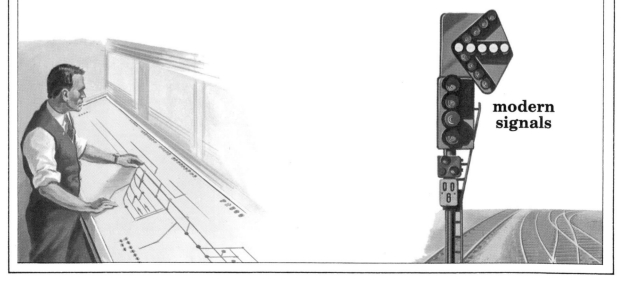

modern
signals

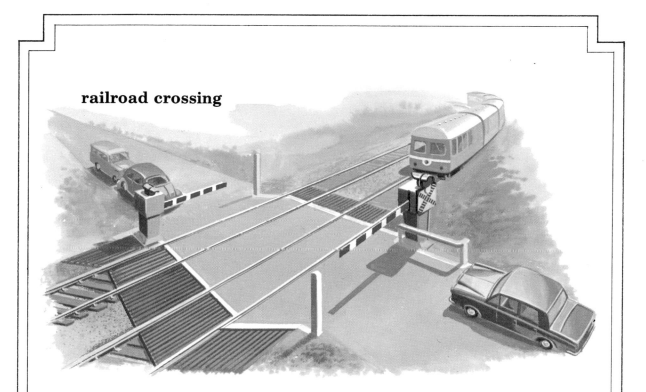

railroad crossing

Sometimes railroad tracks cross roads. These places are called railroad crossings. When a train comes near the crossing, a bell rings. Gates come down across the road, and lights flash warning. Drivers stop at the crossing. They wait until the train has passed. Then the gates go up, and the lights stop flashing. The railroad crossing is clear. Drivers move across the tracks.

Railroad tracks must be tested with care often. Even small cracks in the rail can cause accidents. Special machines test and clean the rails. In cold weather, heaters are used to keep railroad tracks from freezing.

testing tracks

Sometimes trains have accidents.
Engines or cars go off the rails. Big cranes
are used to clear the track. If the track has
been damaged, it must be repaired quickly.
Other trains are waiting to use the tracks.

crane

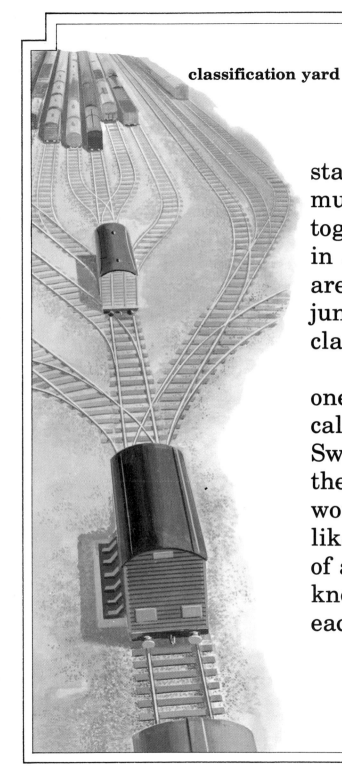

classification yard

Before a train starts out, its cars must be joined together. This is done in a yard where there are many tracks and junctions. It is called a classification yard.

Moving cars from one track to another is called switching. Switching is done by the yardmaster. He works in a building like the control tower of an airport. He knows the location of each car in the yard.

oil car

Freight cars haul different things. They may carry coal or bricks or concrete. Some carry oil or gasoline. Others haul animals.

Some goods are packed in freight containers. These containers can be lifted wth a crane from a train to a truck or ship.

freight container
being lifted

The first passenger cars had no roofs. The people sat close together. Smoke from the engine blew in their faces. Later, railroad cars were built with roofs and windows. They were more comfortable.

early passenger car

Today trains have comfortable seats. The cars are warm in winter and cool in summer. Some train trips take days. So trains have restaurants and sleeping cars. Passengers on some modern trains can even make telephone calls.

modern passenger car

suspension railroad

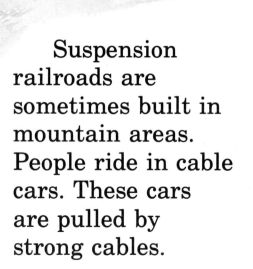

Suspension railroads are sometimes built in mountain areas. People ride in cable cars. These cars are pulled by strong cables.

cog railroad

Cog railroads are built up steep hills or slopes. The track has rungs like a ladder. The train has a cogwheel. This is a wheel with teeth. As the cogwheel turns, the teeth fit into the rungs of the ladder. The train moves up or down the hill. The engine is built so that it stays level on the slope.

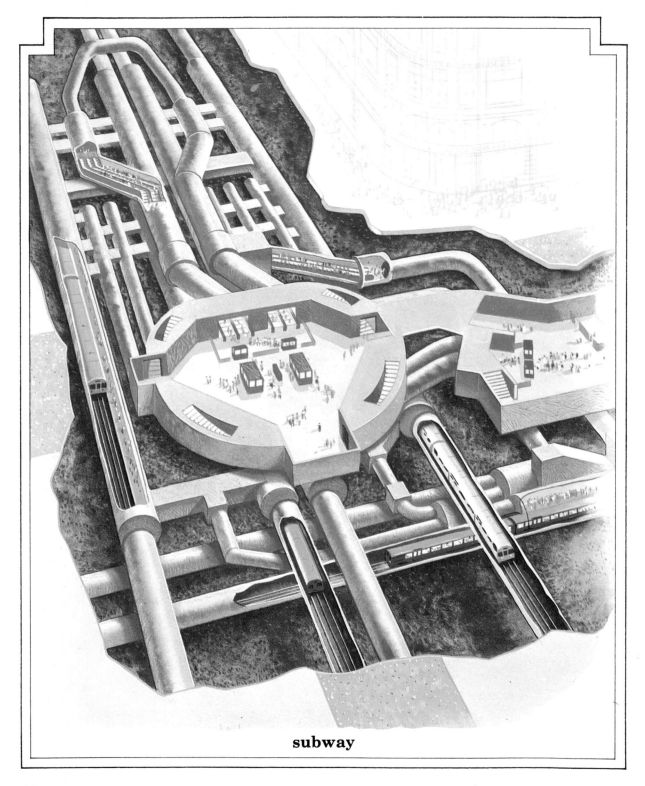

subway

Many big cities have railroads that run under the streets. These railroads are often called subways. Some stations are also underground. People take stairs from the street down to the station.

Paris has a famous subway. It is called the Metro. Its trains run quietly on rubber tires.

Stations of the Moscow subway are grand. They look like rooms in a palace.

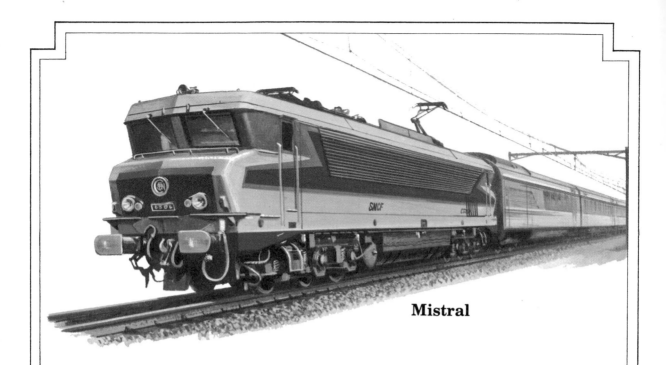

Mistral

Many trains today are electric. They are cleaner and faster than steam trains.

One of the most famous electric trains is in France. This express train is called the Mistral. The locomotive of the Mistral can go faster than 200 miles per hour (322 kilometers per hour).

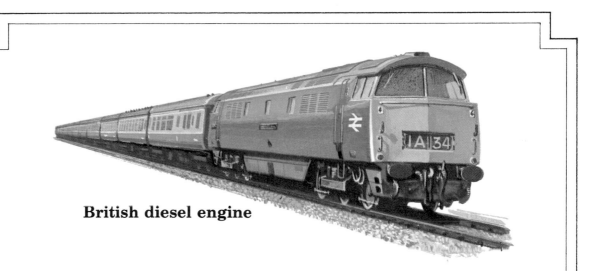

British diesel engine

Some modern trains are pulled by diesel engines. Diesel engines run on fuel oil. They are refueled from pumps just like autos.

Canadian diesel engine

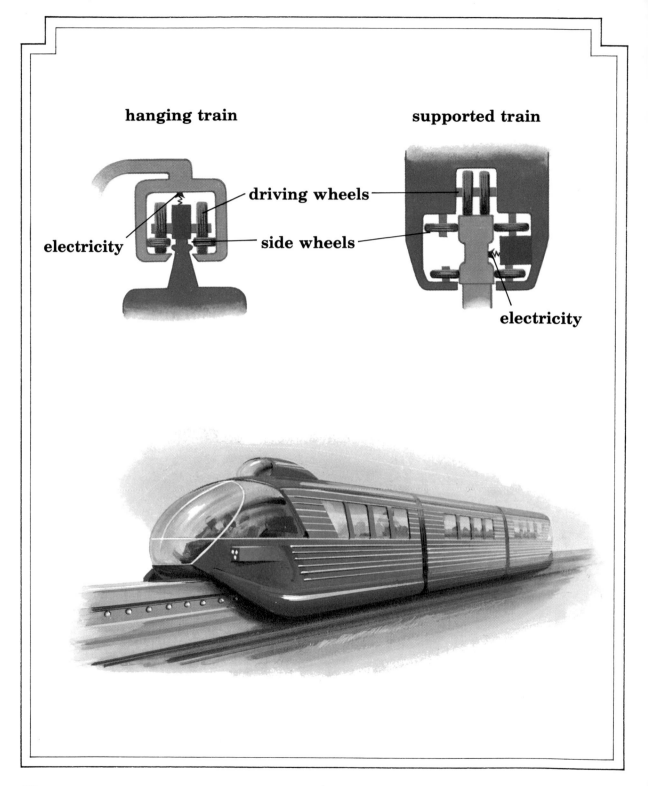

hanging train

supported train

driving wheels

side wheels

electricity

electricity

Monorails are electric trains that run on one rail. One kind of monorail hangs from the rail. All monorails have small driving wheels. These wheels move along a concrete beam. Side wheels keep the train steady. Monorails have rubber tires. That makes them run very quietly.

Someday trains may be suspended above the tracks by magnetism. Another future train is one that would ride above the ground on a cushion of air.

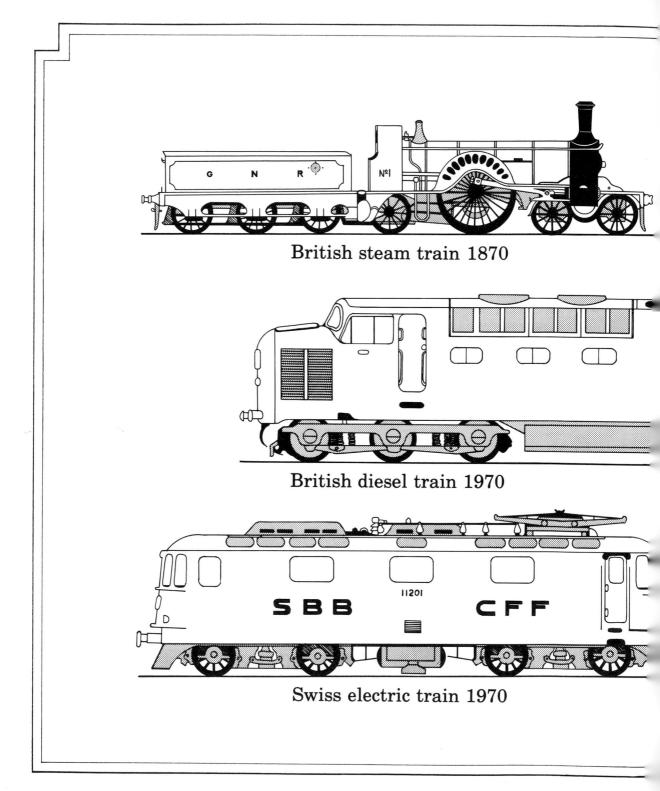

British steam train 1870

British diesel train 1970

Swiss electric train 1970

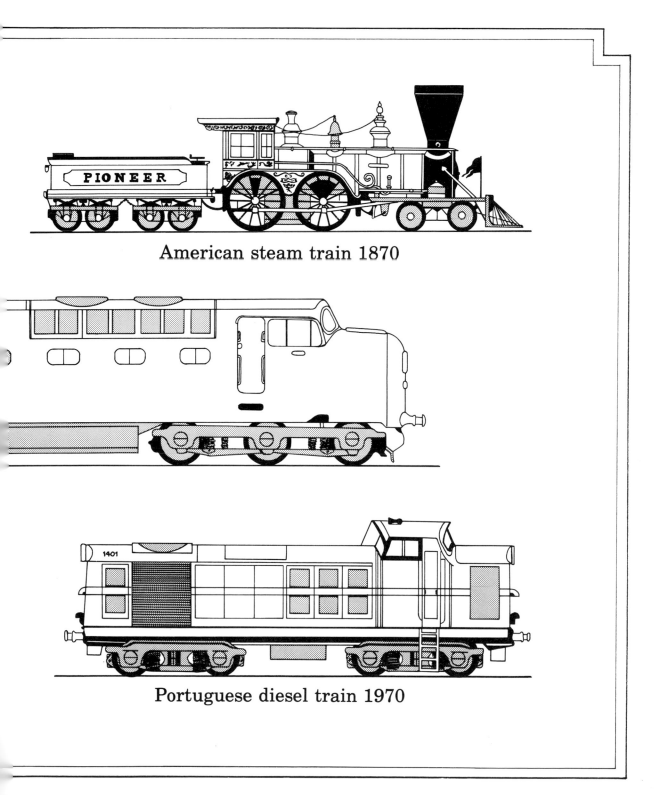

American steam train 1870

Portuguese diesel train 1970

The Metric System

In the United States, things are measured in inches, pounds, quarts, and so on. That system is called the American system. Most other countries of the world use centimeters, kilograms, and liters to measure those things. That system is called the metric system.

At one time the United States was going to change to the metric system. That is why you will see both systems of measurement in some books. For example, you might see a sentence like this: "That bicycle wheel is 27 inches (69 centimeters) across."

Most books you use will have only one system of measurement. You may want to change from one system to the other. The chart on the next page will help you.

All you have to do is multiply the unit of measurement in Column 1 by the number in Column 2. Your answer will be the unit in Column 3.

Suppose you want to change 15 centimeters to inches. First, find *centimeters* in Column 1. Next, multiply 15 times .4. The answer you get is 6. So, 15 centimeters equal 6 inches.

Column 1	Column 2	Column 3
THIS UNIT OF MEASUREMENT	TIMES THIS NUMBER	GIVES THIS UNIT OF MEASUREMENT
inches	2.54	centimeters
feet	30.	centimeters
feet	.3	meters
yards	.9	meters
miles	1.6	kilometers
ounces	28.	grams
pounds	.45	kilograms
fluid ounces	.03	liters
pints	.47	liters
quarts	.95	liters
gallons	3.8	liters
centimeters	.4	inches
meters	1.1	yards
kilometers	.6	miles
grams	.035	ounces
kilograms	2.2	pounds
liters	33.8	fluid ounces
liters	2.1	pints
liters	1.06	quarts
liters	.26	gallons

Where to Read About Trains and Railroads

Pronunciation Key

a	a as in **cat, bad**
ā	a as in **able**, ai as in **train**, ay as in **play**
ä	a as in **father, car**, o as in **cot**
e	e as in **bend, yet**
ē	e as in **me**, ee as in **feel**, ea as in **beat**, ie as in **piece**, y as in **heavy**
i	i as in **in, pig**, e as in **pocket**
ī	i as in **ice, time**, ie as in **tie**, y as in **my**
o	o as in **top**, a as in **watch**
ō	o as in **old**, oa as in **goat**, ow as in **slow**, oe as in **toe**
ô	o as in **cloth**, au as in **caught**, aw as in **paw**, a as in **all**
oo	oo as in **good**, u as in **put**
o͞o	oo as in **tool**, ue as in **blue**
oi	oi as in **oil**, oy as in **toy**
ou	ou as in **out**, ow as in **plow**
u	u as in **up, gun**, o as in **other**
ur	ur as in **fur**, er as in **person**, ir as in **bird**, or as in **work**
yo͞o	u as in **use**, ew as in **few**
ə	a as in **again**, e as in **broken**, i as in **pencil**, o as in **attention**, u as in **surprise**
ch	ch as in **such**
ng	ng as in **sing**
sh	sh as in **shell, wish**
th	th as in **three, bath**
<u>th</u>	th as in **that, together**

GLOSSARY

These words are defined the way they are used in this book

accident (ak′ sə dənt) something that is not expected; when a train breaks down or leaves the track

airport (er′ pôrt′) a place where planes take off and land

cable (kā′ bəl) a thick, strong wire or rope

celebration (sel ə brā′ shən) ceremonies in honor of a special happening

chain (chān) a row of metal links that are joined together

classification (klas′ ə fi kā′ shən) arrangement in groups

coal (kōl) a substance, usually black, that is used as fuel

coast (kōst) the land next to the sea; the east or west coast of the United States

cog (kog) a tooth-shaped part of the rim of a wheel

cogwheel (kog′ hwēl) a wheel with cogs all around the edge or rim

concrete (kon′ krēt) a hard mixture of cement, pebbles, sand, and water

container (kən tā′ nər) an object made to hold something else inside of it

control (kən trōl′) having to do with power or the ability to direct something

cowcatcher (kou′ kach ər) a metal frame on the front of a locomotive that pushes things off the track

crack (krak) a narrow break or split

crane (krān) a large machine used to lift heavy objects

damage (dam′ ij) to break or hurt in some way

electric (i lek′ trik) run by electricity

electricity (i lek tris′ ə tē) a basic source of power; electric current

engine (en′ jin) a machine that makes use of energy to run other machines

famous (fā′ məs) being known to many people

freeze (frēz) to harden or be covered
   with ice because of the cold

freight (frāt) goods or supplies that
   are carried from one place to another

fuel (fyoo′ əl) something that is
   burned to provide power

gasoline (gas ə lēn′) a liquid fuel

golden (gōld′ ən) made of gold

grand (grand) large and impressive

heater (hē′ tər) something that gives heat

invent (in vent′) to make something
   for the first time

junction (jungk′ shən) a place where
   things meet; the place where one
   railroad track meets another

kilometers per hour (ki lom′ ə tərz pur
   our) a speed measured by the number
   of kilometers something travels in
   one hour

locomotive (lō′ kə mō′ tiv) an engine
   that pulls the cars of a railroad train

miles per hour (mīlz pur our′) a speed
   that is measured by the number of miles

something travels in one hour

modern (mod′ ərn) belonging to the present; up to date

monorail (män′ ə rāl′) a train that runs on a single track

passenger (pas′ ən jər) someone who is taken from one place to another in a vehicle

pump (pump) a machine used to move liquids, especially fuel, from one place to another

rail (rāl) the narrow metal bar on which a train moves

railroad (rāl′ rōd′) the rails a train runs on; the whole system of trains, tracks, and stations

record (rek′ ərd) a performance that is better than any other

refuel (rē fyoo′ əl) to fill something again with fuel

repair (ri per′) to fix something; to make something work correctly

restaurant (res′ tər ənt) a place where
  food is served to people at tables
ridge (rij) a thin, raised strip
rung (rung) a narrow strip joining the
  sides of a ladder or the rails of a
  railroad track
semaphore (sem′ ə fôr′) a way to give
  messages to trains by moving signals near
  the track
slope (slōp) ground that rises at an angle
speed (spēd) a rate of motion; quick
  or fast motion
spike (spīk) a long, heavy nail
stairs (sterz) steps which lead from
  one level of a place to another
steam (stēm) the water vapor given off
  when water is boiled; being run by steam
steel (stēl) a strong metal made from
  iron and carbon
subway (sub′ wā′) an electric railroad
  which runs under the ground, usually
  found in cities

suspension railroad (sə spen′ shən
rāl′ rōd) a railroad that runs up
steep hills or mountains and uses cars
that hang from cables

switch (swich) to move trains from
one track to another

tires (tīrz) the rubber part around
the rim of a wheel

track (trak) rails that trains run on

underground (un′ dər ground′) under
the surface of the earth

upright (up′ rīt′) straight up

Bibliography

Barton, Byron. *Trains*. New York: T.Y. Crowell, 1986.

Broekel, Ray. *Trains*. Chicago: Childrens Press, 1981.

Cave, Ron and Joyce. *What About Trains?* New York: Gloucester Press, 1982.

Hamer, Mick. *Transport*. New York: Franklin Watts, 1982.

Herda, D.J. *Model Railroads*. New York: Franklin Watts, 1982.

Marshall, Ray and John Bradley. *The Train: Watch It Work*. New York: Viking-Penguin, Inc., 1986.

Sheffer, H.R. *Trains*. Mankato, Minnesota: Crestwood House, 1982.

Vialls, Christine. *The Industrial Revolution Begins*. Minneapolis: Lerner Publications, 1982.